Dr. Angela Fetzner

Communication
with animals

Touching an
animal's soul

Translated by
Phil Stanway

Imprint

© 2020 by Dr. Angela Raab née Fetzner
all rights reserved
1st Edition 2020

Translation by Phil Stanway
original german title „Tierkommunikation"

Coverdesign:
ZERO agency, Munich
using motives from shutterstock.com
Coverphoto: © Michael Raab
Book set: Michael Raab

ISBN: 9798673281970
Imprint: Independently published

Contents

„The love for all living creatures is the most noble attribute of man."
(Charles Darwin)

This page is intentionally left blank, because the photos and pictures printed always on the right side inside the printed version of these book!

Communication with animals – an intense level of contact

Many of us speak with animals, but communicating with animals calls for a different kind of contact and interaction. The communication is not through words but is rather a kind of telepathy or exchange on the plane of thought.

The point is to understand how an animal views its situation or to find out what may be affecting its health. As the animal's companion, you try to share its level of experience and to see the world through its eyes from its own point of view.

In communication with animals, a role is played by not only the heart but also the soul. The communication takes place on the plane of the subconscious, which expresses itself through images, feelings, hues and impressions. Even words and phrases may be exchanged but they are not spoken but rather communicated from mind to mind.

In other words, it is not a matter of telling your dog what he should do or of telling your cat how lovely she is. It is also not a matter of interpreting the body language of your dog, donkey or horse. Naturally, this is crucial in getting along with an animal on a daily basis but is not the essence of communicating with animals.

The essence rather consists in experiencing how an animal is feeling, how it perceives something or why it is behaving in a certain way. There may be something which it finds problematic or is unable to understand and which, if it seems to be disturbing, affects the animal's behavior. Communicating with the animal may then bring the problem to light and reveal whether he is in pain or suffering from something else.

**Respect me
as I respect you**

It may even be useful in searching for him, if he is nowhere to be seen.

It may even be possible to communicate with a deceased animal, whose soul has simply left its body and is now on another plane.

Communication with an animal is not one-sided, as animals may also wish to understand us. An intense exchange on the plane of the soul and heart, of perception and emotion, can help to make life more harmonious. It helps animals and their companions to get along with each other better on a daily basis. It is often amazing what animals have to communicate. Their ability to perceive and judge situations may be less complex but it is often unprejudiced and accurate.

The fact that their reactions are fairly simple may not reflect their level of intelligence. What animals wish to express may not be naive or silly. More often, they assess situations clearly and express their judgments directly and relevantly.

Indeed, at times they even reveal a typical humor, which many of us would not expect from our pets or any other animal. Some animals even show notable pragmatism and are able to express a wide range of emotions. They may let us see what they see, how they see it and what they feel about it. This can also be a help if we are trying to find them.

The other way round, a person may try to let an animal look at the world through his own eyes too. He can try to let it know why he is acting in a certain way, especially towards the animal. These reciprocal efforts lead to a better, deeper and more compassionate understanding on both sides and help their relationship to become more balanced and trusting.

Communication with animals – prerequisites and background

Basically, we are all able to communicate with animals, and the animals themselves are able to communicate with us. The reason is quite simple: every person and every animal has its own inner world or soul, and souls can enter directly into contact with one another and exchange information. The difficulty for humans lies in trying to do without their usual forms of communication and thought for the sake of communicating on a different plane.

The most important prerequisite is respect for the animal as a living and equally worthy creature. Every animal has its own personality and is not necessarily inferior to a human in its thoughts and feelings. This is true of an ant, a dog, a bird or an elephant. We are just more familiar with some kinds of animals than with others, each of which works well in its own way.

Certainly, we may find it easier to see the world through the eyes of a dog or cat than through the eyes of a grass hopper, but communication is possible even with creatures very different in form and behavior.

Donkeys are very sensitive animals.

 11

To communicate with animals you have to be open-minded. You have to be ready to meet an animal on its own level and to listen to it patiently. You have to accept it as an independent and worthy companion. Many of us would be amazed what animals sometimes 'say' if they are only allowed to. Animals often have an untainted wisdom which – if recognized by humans – shed a wholly new light on some things.

Listen to us, we have so much to say

My donkeys: Achiel (light grey) and Harrie (dark grey)

Why communicate with animals, soul to soul?

We sometimes want to have a better understanding of animals because things are not going smoothly. A cat may be unclean or a dog may behave oddly for no apparent reason, or a donkey may be withdrawn.

Some of these kinds of behavior may be upsetting, but you may still wish an animal well and want to get to the root of a problem.

Questions in need of answers or problems in need of clarification may include the following:

- Does your horse feel comfortable with its saddle? Is it too heavy or does it press into the skin?
- Would your guinea pig prefer to live out in the open or in an enclosure? How would it like its surroundings to be arranged?
- How does your dog feel if you take him for a walk on a lead? Does he prefer to have a collar or a harness, and why?
- What is your cat fretting about? Why is she so finicky with her food? And why is she loath to use her toilet?
- Is your pet in pain?
- Is your pet afraid?
- Has it been traumatized in the past?
- Why does your donkey balk at certain situations?
- Why does your donkey kick out?

Sometimes, however, everything is going smoothly and we are just curious about an animal and would like see the world through its eyes.

We may wish to know, for instance, how a cat feels on hunting for mice or may wish to learn the secret of its success; or we may wish to know a dog's feelings on being taken for a walk or on sniffing in the undergrowth or even what the world looks like to a guinea pig.

We may also wonder whether the owner of dog freely decides whether or not to offer the dog a tidbit or whether the dog telepathically slips the thought into his mind. It may more often be the case than is widely supposed that a dog prompts its owner. The idea just pops up in the owner's mind for no evident reason, then the tidbit is handed over and no questions are asked.

If an animal is plainly unwell or sick, it should be taken to a doctor, but we may nonetheless usefully ask it about the cause of its suffering, instead of relying wholly on a professional diagnosis. This is especially true if a psychological factor is involved or if an animal has recently been traumatized. If it has recently been acquired, the trauma may not be known to his owner, but if it were, the owner could take appropriate action.

We may also usefully appreciate the full range of an animal's feelings. It is often very hard for an animal to make its feelings clear to a person or for a person to find his way into an animal's world of experience. An acquired ability to communicate with an animal may make things so much easier. Apart from making it easier to answer certain questions or to solve certain problems, it can help to establish and maintain a better friendship.

© depositphotos - Hannamariah
Sad dog

Communication with animals involves telepathy

Many pets are well known to react reliably to their owners' unexpressed feelings. Their feelings and thoughts may not be expressed in words, but they affect other creatures around them. Indeed the word *telepathy* comes from the ancient Greek τῆλε tēle (at a distance) und πάθος (pathos or empathy), so it alludes to the ability to sense others' thoughts and feelings without relying on ears and eyes.

Whether or not we mean to, we continually affect creatures around us through our thoughts and feelings, though we may seldom notice. To communicate with an animal, we deliberately shift onto this plane of interaction and open ourselves up to what the animal is feeling and would like to 'say'. This also lets us explain things to an animal, to send it a simple message or to pose a practical question.

You may even be intuitive in general and some-times have the impression that you are sharing your pet's feelings, not by interpreting gestures but rather from heart to heart or from soul to soul. This may be only a casual impression for which you have no ready explanation. You may feel that your animal is ill at ease with its si-tuation, has certain aches and pains or is upset about something or other. Then, how useful it is to be able to communicate with him, albeit without words! In the course of time, this non-verbal communication intensifies and can be applied more consciously and precisely. Even if you are convinced that you have no aptitude for this, you are sure to have the ability to some extent and be able to make progress.

Are you familiar with the following situation? You happen to meet a stranger, and from the start you feel at ease or ill at ease. You have no clear reason why but the impression is crystal clear. This in itself is a kind of telepathy. The stranger has a certain ambiance which you are able to feel clearly or too clearly.

The same thing happens to many people on entering a room, where they sense a tense, tetchy or relaxing atmosphere. Another pleasant and common example is that you are just thinking of someone, when he suddenly rings up or sends a message. People who have a lot to do with each other often start to say the same thing at the same time. These are all instances of telepathy.

In living with animals, we sometimes find that our dogs or horses react to something we have in mind but have yet to express. You may want to lead your dog to something or may want to stop your horse, then before you have given a sign, the animal obeys.

It also works the other way round. Your pet may want you to do something, and you promptly oblige, as if it were your own idea. It is sometimes not at all easy to find out whether an idea is really yours or your pet's, telepathically conveyed. Communication with animals can also help you to find this out, be it to satisfy your idle curiosity or to find out who is wearing the trousers!

© Michael Raab

My donkeys Achiel and Harrie always have something to say and sometimes they like to be bossy.

21

Some facets and aims of communication with animals

Communication with animals depends on an exchange of images, sensations, feelings and thoughts. It takes place without words on a plane of energy, from heart to heart and from soul to soul. Nonetheless, people who communicate with animals also receive messages including words. They are not verbal messages sent as such by the animals, as shown by the fact that a message from a foreign animal is not in its own language but the language of the recipient. The message is received by the recipient's subconscious then translated into familiar words.

For instance an animal may let its owner share its anxiety, or the words 'Let's get out of here!' may pop into its owner's mind.

© depositphotos - conrad.levac
There is also communication by gazing

 23

It is important for an animal and its owner to learn more about each other. An ability to communicate with an animal may help you to understand why it is acting differently or oddly. It may offer you a clue as to why an animal has run away or vanished or even a clue as to where it is now. The animal in turn may may receive a hint from you, as to whether it should stay put, give a sign of its presence or simply come back. A person good at communicating with animals can sense whether an absent animal is feeling all right or is wounded or even in mortal danger.

In the case of an animal recently deceased, this kind of communication may let you accompany its soul into the afterlife. It may also help the animal to put its past behind it and to overcome any shock involved in the transition. This may ease the feelings of both the animal and its owner, as parting is sweet sorrow to both. You maybe loath to let your pet go forth into the afterlife alone and may wish to accompany it for awhile, to explain how it happened to die. If it died through being put to sleep, you may wish to explain why this seemed to be advisable under the circumstances. This may be a relief to you as well as to your animal. However, it may also be a good idea to communicate with an animal before deciding between life and death, to find out whether or not its pains are greater than its love of life. A medic can rely only on guesswork.

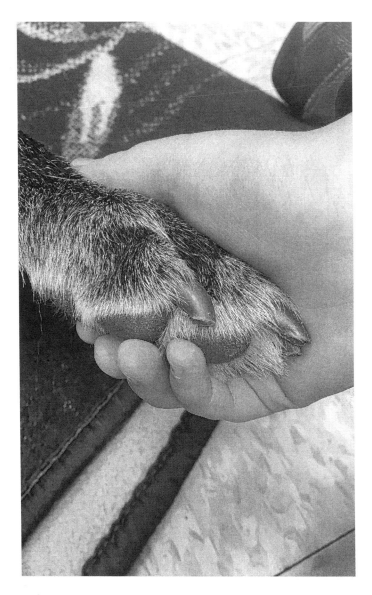

ne last moment with a dog before it is put to sleep. Even communication with a deceased animal is possible.

 25

Sometimes an animal is asked whether or not it is angry with its owner. The latter may wonder whether it may excuse a poor decision affecting it. Maybe the owner wished to do it a favor, by offering it a different delicacy or by cycling ahead of it, unaware that it is allergic to certain foods or that it suffers from arthritis and is unable to keep up with a bicycle.

Sometimes the soul of a deceased animal is worried about friends it has left behind. Here too, communication may help. There are many reasons for resolving to communicate with animals, whether an animal is in this world or the next.

All in all, it can be said that communicating with animals is a way to let animals and humans understand and get along with each other more easily. It lets them appreciate each other more intimately, accommodate each other more fully and bond with each other more firmly. Communication with an animal lets an owner offer support in difficult situations and explain unpleasant decisions. It lets an animal know why some rules of behavior are important to humans and that he has not been casually abandoned if finally put to sleep. There are countless situations in which it is useful to be able to point things out.

Life from an animal's point of view

How can this kind of communication work at all? After all, it can hardly be grasped intellectually or verbalized. It is hard to imagine and is mysterious to the point of being elusive.

Basically, you open yourself to the nature and essence of the animal whom you would like to communicate with. You let your inner self get in touch with the animal's inner self. You can then share information about your points of view, your worlds of feeling and experience, your ways of perceiving things and your criteria of judgment. In effect, you let an animal speak for itself.

For this to work, it is important to calm down physically and mentally. Free yourself from everyday concerns and possible disturbance. The subconscious needs a certain scope and can hardly achieve it in the midst of scurrying thoughts.

The state needed is rather like sleep. Your conscious mind comes to rest, then impressions may surface in the form of daydreams, or you let your thoughts drift over events of the day and anything else of concern,, though if you are too self-centered, you can pay little attention to an animal.

For the sake of achieving a suitable state, you are free to use anything helpful. Candles may create a peaceful ambiance, as may the scent of incense or the sound of meditative music. Shamans use drums to calm the mind, whereas yogis have a whole range of exercises involving breathing and postures. You may best find out for yourself what works for you.

Understanding and being understood

There follows a simple example from the life of a dog, to show what it may be like. You can apply it in a suitable form to other problems with other animals.

A dog becomes part of your family for the first time and is still unfamiliar with you and his new surroundings. You on the other hand forced yourself upon him. You fastened him to a lead and took him with you into a car, where he was placed on a wobbly seat with the purr of a motor and odd scents. He had little inkling of what was happening, but finally the wobbling stopped and he was taken out of the car and led to a different building, which he had never seen before. New scents, sounds and sights converged on him from all sides, but he had no idea how to react or why he was there. He is still perplexed and wondering how to deal with you, but in such unnatural surroundings, he is unable to rely on his hunches.

At some point of the proceedings, he is fastened to the lead once more and taken outside. Once more, he has no inkling of where he is and why and is told in an alien tongue to relieve himself. To him it is all gobbledygook, so he carefully refrains from doing anything, till finally he is taken back indoors.

Relieved to be off the lead once more, he promptly relieves his bladder or gut then runs to and fro, afraid to fall asleep at night.

The next day, he is taken outside again for no apparent reason then is again brought in, wondering what the rituals mean.

Later the same morning, he is put back into the car, which again purrs and wobbles, till it finally stops and he is taken into another building, as unnatural and mysterious as the first, which is due to be his home, though no one has informed him of the fact.

Once more, he is faced by weird figures, who grab him and examine him with various instruments. He is being medically examined, perhaps for no better reason than the fact that he has been so restless and irregular in his behavior. Hands grab him and something pricks him like the tooth of a snake, so he tries to wriggle free or to dissolve into thin air but is firmly restrained. His suspicion of being abducted into alien territory is dramatically confirmed.

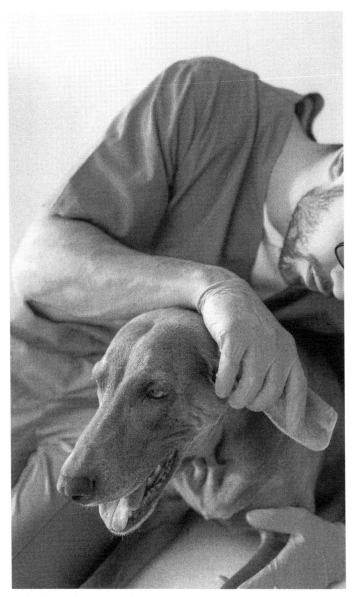

A dog being medically checked. A very odd situation for almost any animal.

 31

After these gratuitous and frightening events, he is led back to the car and locked in, till he is back in the family home, which is now more familiar but still unsettling. His nervousness is evident, so he is ordered to take it easy, but he is unable to understand the order so empties his bladder and gut, to be on the safe side, then on being taken outside, he only trots with his tail between his legs. On meeting other strange people and strange dogs, he would like to flee, and on passing a parked car, he veers away and stays at a safe distance. By now he now knows only too well that cars are there for whisking dogs away to alien territory, and the less he has of that, the better. As for the contents of smelly garbage bins at intervals along his way, he would rather not look into them more deeply.

Things like this are commonplace experiences for a dog brought from elsewhere, but on being first experienced they are new and bewildering, and the dog may have had earlier, more harrowing experiences before being brought to a home. Whelps may also feel very upset, if taken away from their brothers, sisters and mother and left alone.

© depositphotos - petertt
A dog in a car. Give your dog time to get used to it.

 33

Naturally, not all dogs are alike. Some are more daring and self-confident and eager to explore new surroundings, but this too may have its drawbacks. The dogs may bite and tug at everything in sight, including their owners, if the latter come too close to their food or would like to fasten them to their leads.

Indeed, there is a wide range of behavior due on the one hand to different inherited dispositions and on the other hand to different experiences. These include not only their past socialization but also their present surroundings and the people there. Given all these factors, it may be hard for an owner to guess why a dog is behaving in a certain way and resisting all efforts to change it. The owner may be sympathetic but nonetheless soon at his wit's end, and dealing with the dog may become risky or even dangerous. If the dog takes his frustration out on the antique furniture, not only the dog but also his owner may begin to behave oddly, and barking for hour after hour may bother not only the owner but also elderly neighbors and the police.

In most cases, the animal and his human owner or companion get used to the notion of sharing a home and having to compromise with each other, but compromises depend on mutual understanding. Each needs at least a rough notion of what the other would like to gain or is willing to yield. They have to be able to see things through each other's eyes. Being better informed may not be enough but at least be a step on the right path, so there is a need for communication. This may be due to a situation like the one outlined above or to something else. The problems may have to do with health, traumas, wishes, needs, misunderstandings and so on. Communication with an animal is always useful if either the human or the animal would like to be put in the picture.

Training or communication?

If a dog behaves like the one above, it is taken to be disturbed. Of course, the problem may be quite different, as the dog may snap at others, chase cats, leap at joggers, be loath to be left alone, be scruffy, bark at cars or terrorize other pets on the principle that the best means of defense is attack. Still, many odd kinds of behavior are due only to health problems yet to be recognized.

Whatever the problem, cats, horses, donkeys, rodents, birds, pigs or goats are like dogs in having their personal or individual characteristics, due partly to their experiences and surroundings and partly to how they have been able to come to terms with them. Their reactions to situations become habitual, as do the reactions of wild animals, who learn from their parents, adapt to their surroundings and learn from other experiences.

No animals are problematic as such. We just have to heed what animals would like us to know.

If an animal behaves problematically, this only means that there is friction between the animal and its owner for reasons still unclear or hard to avoid, so relations are continually strained. In the case of the dog described above, there is a pattern of behavior unexpected by its owners, so they find it hard to fathom and deal with.

Most socialized dogs try to avoid conflicts, though some may aggressively stand their ground without any sign of restraint or appeasement, but sometimes a situation is unavoidable in a modern human society. If a dog is unwilling to face up to it, owners all too often assume that they have only to bring it round to their own point of view, then it will change its behavior. But the dog may have little knowledge of the human point of view, and its owners may have little knowledge of the dog's. In such cases there are:

Three possible approaches

- The human partner seeks a solution.
- Both partners resign themselves to perpetual conflict.
- The human views the animal as beyond redemption.

If a human resolves to seek a solution for a dog, he may take the dog to a trainer. There are plenty of trainers for dogs, quite a number for cats and horses, and even some for donkeys. Trainers try in various ways, to influence an animal's behavior. They try to let an animal know what he is expected to do or not to do. If he behaves properly, he should feel the appreciation, and if not, he should feel the disappointment. Ignorance too should evoke a suitable reaction. Desired behavior can be learned, by offering an animal choices and by rewarding him for choosing the right one. A dog can even learn gradually not to be afraid of certain things such as cars or of being taken for rides.

New Year's Eve (at least in Germany, on account of fireworks) is frightening to many animals, especially to those who react mostly to sounds, but an animal can also be taught not to panic. This can be done by helping it to associate the occasion with happy experiences too or by distracting it, if it seems to be especially worried about something. In the long run, it may then be less nervous in general.

Such training may be important and proper, if the trainer is apt and competent, but what often remains overlooked is an animal's inner world, where the causes of its behavior are to be found. This is where communicating with an animal is useful, as it lets the animal speak for itself, be it without words. Just being offered a chance to communicate is often a great relief to an animal. It may feel that someone is finally taking it seriously and that the effort of communication is worth it.

It should be allowed to express how it feels, how it experiences events and people around it and to explain its behavior. Its owner may wish to explain odd human behavior and how humans would like animals to treat them. Naturally, an animal too should feel free to express its wishes and needs and be assured that this is acceptable. A person and animal can thereby get to know each other more closely and find a way to overcome pitfalls or to harmonize their aims. It is often easier for a person or animal to accept a certain kind of behavior if aware of what is behind it.

© depositphotos - cynoclub

Training an animal. A difficult decision. Make sure that your trainer is competent!

If an animal has run away or vanished, it may be possible to sense what has happened to it. If it has died, it may be relieved to say farewell in its own way and to sum up its feelings about life. A person may also be able to ease the passing away of an animal by accompanying it in spirit for awhile. In situations like this, neither cool reasoning nor an animal trainer is much of a help.

It is sometimes practical to use both training and communication at the same time, as an animal may be loath to change its behavior unless given a good reason. There may also be good reasons why an animal is behaving oddly, so they should be discovered and taken into account. After all, an animal has its instincts and experiences and can hardly jump over its own shadow. In such cases, recourse to communicating with an animal has the advantage that the animal does not feel coerced into doing something unreasonable or risky so is more likely to oblige. Of course, this is true of animals in general, not only of dogs.

© depositphotos - wollertz

If an animal runs away, there is sure to be a good reason. Try to find it!

 43

What communication with animals is *not* for

Communication with an animal lets the animal speak for itself, if not in words. It lets the animal reveal its needs and point of view, and lets a person reveal his in a way intelligible to the animal. The animal can thereby learn why the person is behaving in a certain way and why he expects the animal to do the same. The main reason may simply be to achieve a harmonious coexistence and to let the animal be accepted into human society with its rules and habits.

Another reason for trying to influence an animal's behavior may be concern for safety in traffic, and yet another be the fact that an owner cannot always keep an eye on a pet, so a pet may sometimes have to care for itself. A dog may also have to be on a lead or have a cage round its mouth or be taken to a medic for an injection or for protection against parasites. A new cat may have to be kept indoors, till it has settled down, and may even have to spend a day indoors later, if a hunt is taking place in neighboring fields or if fireworks are being let off for a celebration, as at the new year in Germany or on bonfire night in England.

There are many simple rules and regulations which are self-evident to most humans but are weird or even crazy to animals.

© depositphotos - ViktoriaNov44
The risks of roads are not clear to dogs. Here too, training is needed.

 45

But even if an animal becomes aware of our likes and dislikes, it may not automatically accept them, letting us lean back and get on with our own lives. An animal may understand why his owner is living in certain surroundings and behaving in certain ways without feeling that he as a pet should do the same. The aim of communication is mainly to establish a broader base of agreement.

A dog, donkey or horse may not be able to overcome a traumatic experience as soon as his new owner kindly points out that the danger has passed and is unlikely to return in the near future. Were persuasion as simple as that, and were inner thoughts and feelings so easily redirected, even we as humans would find it easy to stay on an even keel. We would no longer be tossed hither and thither by anxiety and depression like rafts on a rough sea. Any distraught person would only have to be told that everything is fine, to be bright and sunny.

Since persuasion is less simple, there is a need for socialization, to cope with everyday life and the world around us, and there is also a need for practice and habituation. Basically, we should not take everything for granted but also resort to measures helping an animal to adapt.

© depositphotos - gezafarkas - wild donkeys - Donkeys are good-natured and clever and can be domesticated in the course of a few generations. They are then reliable companions for people..

Communication with an animal makes it much easier to uncover the immediate and underlying causes of friction. It lets us see the world through the animal's eyes and to take its character into account when trying to train it, then friction can be lessened and the animal be fitted more comfortably into its situation, as communication helps the animal to grasp the situation and the aims of its owner better. It can then try to be more obliging, then the two of them can move on together, hand in hand or paw in paw. They know each other's aims and hopes and work better as a team.

Through communication, a person and an animal can support each other better in many situations, even after one of them has died. Communication alone is unable to solve all problems but helps to solve some. By communicating, you may encourage a vanished cat, perhaps timidly in hiding or inadvertently locked in a shed, to make its location known or to come home. You may learn whether or not a pet is still alive and healthy or is wounded, in need of help.

Donkeys and even horses never shake hands or hooves but rather touch each other with their heads, nostrils or mouths.f

Every animal has its own personality

When dealing with an animal, an owner may forget that the animal is not only a cat or dog or some other animal but also an individual in its own right. He may all too often focus on whether or not a dog is obedient and a horse reliably heeds prompting. A budgerigar needs company and a big enough cage or home, and a cat may sharpen its claws on a chair or the wallpaper instead of a tree, if these are more readily available. We casually expect lions and elephants in a circus to do as they have been taught and we hope that gnats will kindly avoid us down by a lake. Indeed, bees are less likely to sting us, given a choice between our arms and a meadow of wildflowers.

Many people are superficial in observing and reacting to animals. Most of us realize that one horse is touchier than another, that one dog is milder than another and that cats prefer to lead rather than follow, but that is about it. Whether recognized or not, every animal has its own inner life and fund of experience. This has not only to do with whether it is a cat or a dog, a horse or a donkey or even with the kind of dog and so on. One animal differs from another of the same variety, just as no two people are exactly alike in how they feel and think. Moreover, animals are perceptive and reflective and learn from experience.

This is not to say that each animal is only one of a kind, as this is more the exception than the rule. Mostly, a labrador retriever will happily retrieve, a watchdog willingly watch, and a sheepdog care for sheep, even if left to perform its duty alone. Donkeys tend to be self-willed, dogs to be accommodating, and horses to gather in herds. Some wasps are fiercer than others, according to their kind.

But no particular animal is typical of its group. Even at birth, it has its own leanings and may soon turn out to be shy and withdrawn, though some others in the same group are open and inquisitive. Moreover, in the course of events, each animal goes through a series of experiences not wholly shared by others, comes to terms with these in its own way and translates them into patterns of behavior.

In communicating with animals, you do well to take these differences into account. You may then gain insight into an animal's deepest thoughts and feelings about the world and especially about you, its owner or companion.

Human misconceptions

Suppose you have a dog and often meet a neighbor with a dog. The two dogs greet each other, sniff each other and leap around together. To you, they may seem to be the very best of friends, not only fond of each other but also thrilled whenever they meet. Meanwhile, you share a word or two with your neighbor but otherwise have little to do with him.

One day you happen to meet a different dog, so the dogs circle each other and sniff, while you get to know its owner, a new neighbor. Your familiar neighbor then turns up with her familiar dog, but instead of greeting his own friend with the usual pleasantries, your dog coolly ignores him or even gives him a warning growl then devotes himself to the new dog, whom he invites to play with him.

Someone used to communicating with animals may ask him why he has chosen to snub his old friend. He may then reply indignantly that they were only passing acquaintances. Would you expect such a nuanced reaction from a dog? Perhaps not, but if someone were to ask you about your old neighbor and friend, you would hardly think twice about calling her merely a pleasant neighbor, whose path happens to cross yours at times.

© depositphotos - averyanova
wo dogs play with each other, but they may even fight.

In this respect, your dog is no odder than you. He may be happy to meet and frolic with a certain dog, but a pleasantry is no token of intimacy. There is a line between acquaintance and friendship, whether between people or between dogs.

It is sometimes useful to stand back and to question our lazy assumptions. In case of doubt, we can turn to an animal and ask it non-verbally about them. We may then be surprised to learn that a conflict between an animals and its trainer is due to a factor which has never entered its trainer's head. If an animal is anxious, trembling and rigid, a trainer may tell us to ignore the signs, so as not to let the animal feel that it can thereby gain attention or make its owner yield, whereas an expert may tell us to show pity, or the animal may feel that we are leaving it in the lurch. Given opposite advice by two knowledgeable people, whose advice should we taken and apply? It may be best to turn to the animal itself, to view the situation through its eyes. It too is able to reflect and may have drawn simple but reasonable conclusions.

Sometimes, animals and humans have genuine-
ly different views. Cats free to roam may return
with a mouse or bird, alive or dead, but either
way not in a savory state. Dogs unleashed may
happily play in mud or roll in manure, and a
horse may decide to break into a gallop for the
fun of it, though you are not firmly in the saddle. You may want your donkey to move on, to
be home in time for tea, but the donkey sees
no point in leaving a pleasant place in a hurry.
On the other hand, shared aims are not always
ideal. You may be about to savor your ripe fruit,
when joined by a flight of wasps with the same
aim and enthusiasm.

But, to come back to a dog, who has rubbed its
fur in filth and is bringing it into your home.
You tell him to clean himself first. How would
you react if he told you in words that he has
merely gathered a few natural materials and
that his fur and skin are quite able to cope with
them? He might even feel reasonably offended
about an accusation leveled at him by a person
unwilling to check the evidence. If you would
only wait for the next shower, not only the water but also the smell would be washed away. If
you lack the patience to wait for a shower, you
can go with him for a swim.

If you are trying to get your dog to do something he is afraid to do, your dog might remark that fools rush in where angels fear to tread, or he might ask you why you wish him to risk his, not your neck. If you are hoping to pass an examination with him or to win a prize at a dog exhibition, maybe you should ask him if he too is enthusiastic about the venture. He might reply that he feels less proud of his appearance than of his abilities or that he would rather not try to prove anything to anyone.

The messages which a communicator is able to receive and understand from animals come from the depths of their souls. They may be simple but not shallow or lacking in logic. Animals, according to their personal characteristics, may even have a surprising sense of humor.

In German, a trick for remembering something is known as an *Eselbrücke* or donkey's bridge. This alludes to the fact that donkeys are often afraid to cross bridges over rivers or streams. This is hardly surprising, as donkeys live naturally in barren areas without any streams or rivers to be crossed, so their reluctance to cross bridges is no sign of intransigence but only of their lack of experience. If a donkey is well trained and able to communicate, it may be open to persuasion.

Donkeys live naturally in deserts so are unfamiliar with flowing water. That is why they are loath to go over bridges or to put their hooves into shallows.

How an animal reveals its inner life

Communications with animals have two directions: from you to the animal and the other way round. Communication is about sending or transmitting something and receiving or listening to something in return. Whether consciously or not, we are continually sending out information about our thoughts, moods, feelings and states of health, and animals are continually receiving them. Some of us are intuitively able to receive messages from animals too, to see the world through their eyes and to sense their moods, but mostly we are held back by commonsense or common prejudice, or what we hear and see distracts us from what we intuitively feel.

Certainly we can learn a lot about an animal by observing its behavior and reactions. If only many of us would observe ourselves equally attentively and critically! Sometimes we notice that an animal reacts oddly to certain people or situations in being cheerful, open-minded, inquisitive, aggressive or withdrawn. Sometimes an animal openly displays what the human at its side feels but hesitates to express.

An animal as a person's other half.

Animals are sensitive and often have a very clear notion of what is going on in people's minds. If we are loath to undertake something with an animal, it may sense it and be loath to undertake it with us. We may just be too inattentive or impatient. If you are uncomfortable with someone, your dog may show similar reserve. It may be about to bark at him but then lift a leg, to treat him more politely as a lamppost. Your cat may hiss at certain visitors, or if you have no wish to do any entertaining but prefer not to say so, it may hiss at visitors in general. You own unease may cause your cat or dog to withdraw, your horse to shy or your hens to flap to and fro.

Animals latch on to our thoughts and feelings, understand them and behave accordingly. This applies not only to certain situations but also to things in general. If you deal with life high-handedly, your animal may do the same. How and to what extent it does so depends on itss own personality. Likewise, if you never quite sure how best to behave and are rather withdrawn, your animal may reveal the same inclination, or if you are happy-go-lucky, it may prove to be merry and daring. These parallels are often unnoticed by outsiders, but you know your own thoughts and feelings and can see them faithfully reflected.

It makes things easier if you are able to communicate with animals well and to check more closely in what ways the animal is trying to mimic you. This may also help you to understand its idiodyncracies. In most cases, you are likely to find that the mimicry is due less to a wish to make fun of you than to be like you on account of your close relationship. Unwittingly, the animal reveals to the world what is in you and less openly expressed, as if it were your unofficial spokesman or representative, even if you prefer to be a closed book.

An animal may mirror its owner or human companion to such an extent that if the latter falls ill, the animal too falls ill. You may for instance finish a meal and begin to feel queasy when suddenly your pet throws up. It is sometimes hard to guess whether an animal has been affected by a person or the other way round, but this too can be explored through direct communication.

Being more closely and harmoniously related

If you are fond of an animal, you want it to feel fine and enjoy life and are willing to go to great lengths to ensure that it does. Likewise, if an animal is fond of you, it may be willing to go to similar lengths. But even in such cases, there are sometimes conflicts of interest, areas of friction, differences of opinion and misunderstandings. People try to resolve such issues among themselves by talking them over, viewing a situation from various angles and finding a joint way forward.

With an animal and a person, the situation is less symmetrical, as the person is not only the defendant but also the judge and jury. Whether or not the interests of the animal are duly taken into account depends very much on the person. Certainly some of us come to decisions which we believe are the best for both parties, but often they are based more on our preconceptions than on an animal's real desires. What we claim to know is often merely a potpourri of guesswork, speculation and misinterpretation. Sometimes we hit the nail on the head, but often we hit our thumbs instead or hit an animal's paws.

To harmonize our efforts with those of an animal, we need to know its aims and views. Just trying to train it for the sake of reducing friction is less effective. The training may help to avoid open conflict but this is a far cry from pervasive harmony. The absence of open conflict only means that your animal is trying to make life easier for itself by making life easier for you, but if you want to improve the relationship through love and understanding, you may have to begin by granting it equal rights, including the right to communicate in its own way.

One cause of friction and misunderstanding consists of illness. An animal can hardly say a certain part of his body is hurting or that something is wrong inside him. Even if you have the impression that something is bothering him, it may be hard to guess what it is. The difficulty is due partly to the fact that the bother may be physical or mental, or the one may have led to the other.

If you want to undertake something with your animal, it will surely be more pleasant, if your animal would also like to undertake it with you. There are many reasons for trying to improve such a relationship, especially with farm animals but also with other domestic animals who live with us less closely than dogs and cars. Pigs, cattle, goats, sheep, hens, ducks and geese have inner lives just as we do. Each of them has its own personality and certain abilities, preferences, needs, wishes and points of view.

It is not just more practical to have a better understanding of an animal; it also helps us to have a better and more intense relationship, more fruitful for both sides. This is true of every animal in our lives, as each of them is unique in its own way.

We can do a lot in the company of donkeys, especially going for strolls.
It brings us and the donkeys closer to nature.

Two ways to understand an animal

Communicating with it is not the only way to develop a better understanding of an animal. Apart from having its individual traits, an animal also has traits typical of its kind such as what it tends to like or dislike or how it tends to express itself. What is thrilling to a horse may be dull to a donkey. If a dog is excited, it wags its tail and does so differently according to the nature of its excitement, but if a cat is excited, it expresses the excitement more generally through its body. Owing to these differences, we may best appeal to an animal in suitable ways. Often, an animal's state of mind can be guessed only by taking various aspects of its bodily behavior into account.

This is why there are experts in dogs, others in cats and others in horses, donkeys, wolves and rodents. These experts focus on certain kinds of animals and analyze their behavior, social habits, how they communicate with each other and how they interact with their surroundings. Owing to their familiarity with the animals, they are better able to inform them of how they would like them to behave. This approach is useful, not only for experts but also for the owners or companions of various animals, who would like to get on with them easily and harmoniously.

Trust between a person and an animal is the key to communication.

Besides, if you know an animal well, you more easily notice any significant variation in its behavior, which may be due to a certain problem, a feeling of malaise or an ailment. You can then treat the animal as an individual and deepen your relationship with it and then react more promptly to any friction. You get to know its reactions to people and situations, and your animal gets to know your daily routines and your own reactions. The more you learn about each other on this level of observation, the more easily you can foresee and adapt to each other's behavior.

Of course, you may be tempted to use this to your own advantage, and your animal may do the same. Knowing how you mostly behave, it can more easily persuade you to stroke it or to offer it a tidbit. Likewise, you may realize that your animal reacts more to certain offers, then you can use them as bribes.

However intimate and intense your relationship may become, there may still be friction, snags or ambiguities which you are unable to resolve through all scientific findings and your personal experiences and observations. Sometimes an animal may behave oddly for no obvious reason, and you are unable to guess why.

Sometimes, an animal reveals a lack of trust or confidence in you, and you are unable to convince it that you are reliable and have a firm grasp of the situation. The more you try to do so, the more stubborn or difficult he animal may become and refuse to comply with your requests.

Certainly there are many educational or training methods to make an animal behave in a certain way, but this may be more acceptable to you than to him and merely brush the problem under the carpet. Sooner or later, you may have to face up to the problem. A deep inner familiarity and understanding may be worth seeking and prove to be more rewarding in the long run. Anyone really fond of an animal would like it to be happy and on good terms with its owner, not merely be dragged along as an accessory.

Otherwise, however carefully we observe an animal and however much we learn about it, the animal's own needs and desires are neglected. Animals have as rich an inner world of feelings as our own; they understand the world in their own way, and they try to share their understanding if given a chance.

They are keen to express their wishes, to let others know whether or not they are at ease and to communicate well in general. Some animals of course have limited means of expression so can express less than what they would like to.

Communication from heart to heart and from soul to soul is not subject to these limitations, so it may let an animal and person interact as equals. The inner world of the one can then be sensed and appreciated by the other directly. This may be said to take place on the level of the mind, but the meaning is the same. Different words are often used to describe the same thing.

The special role of communication with animals

This kind of communication lets an animal 'speak' for itself and say what it feels about a relationship, and it also lets its owner explain his own aims and actions. Misunderstandings may otherwise proliferate, as an animal may find it as hard to fathom the odd behavior of a person as a person to fathom that of an animal.

An animal may notice and remember that someone reacts mostly in a certain way to certain situations but be unable to guess why. Animals not only have different needs and habits, they are also used to living in their own very different societies and may be less worried about their image and status than a human is. They have no notion of the rule of law or of opening times, science, politics and the economy.

Animals learn through experience what it is to be treated by a medic and may guess that the treatment has a purpose, though not what the purpose is. Living in the wild has taught them nothing about injections or the use of pills. Often their owners or companions are likewise worried about the outcome of a medical investigation, but this only reinforces their own feeling that things are not going well. After all, if owners are unhappy about a situation, why are they putting their animals into it? In the wild, if a herd as a whole is unsettled, an animal senses that something is wrong and reacts accordingly.

Animals wear no clothes, apart from their own fur, so it is unnatural to a horse to wear a saddle and harness. No dog would think it useful to wear a collar and lead or a basket over its mouth. Dogs appreciate being handed a meal on a plate every day but would like to hunt for themselves too, though their owners are strictly against it. A cat may wonder why its owner throws away every mouse or bird which it manages to catch, only to offer it a meal out of a can. If a cat goes so far as to place a bird dead or wounded in the bed of its owner in the morning as a tasty morsel and if its owner fails to appreciate the gesture, it may find the ingratitude shocking.

Rabbits and similar pets may find it depressing to be kept in only a small pen, though they want to go out and savor the wide world, and birds are accustomed to flying not only from branch to branch but also from land to land, not to hopping around in a cage or to flapping from perch to perch in an aviary. They are unable to understand how and why a barrier has been placed between them and their natural surroundings. A cat may finally learn that its owner objects to its sharpening its claws on wallpaper but not what is sacred about wallpaper. After all, in the wild, it is free to scratch anything it wishes, whether to sharpen its claws or to mark its territory. Why it should use only a piece of wood, not a wall or sofa?

© Michael Raab - The donkey Achiel has chronic obstructive bronchitis. He has gradually got used to this inhalative way of breathing, as it helps him. His fellow donkey, Harrie, is keeping him company.

There is an endless number of similar problems. Animals have not been naturally selected to live with humans and to get along nicely with wallpaper, rugs and furniture, so they instinctively object to human demands which have no apparent use and are very frustrating. If expected to behave unnaturally, they may wish to know why, so an ability to communicate with an animal offers an owner a chance to present his own side of the picture. If an animal is given a chance to pose reasonable questions and to be taken seriously, it may likewise be willing to treat its owner with more respect.

This brings us back to the unique nature of every animal. Even we like to be viewed as a society of individuals, not a set of duplicates. We want to express our personal needs and wishes and to be free to avoid people or situations offensive to us. Communication with our animal companions lets us offer them a chance to express their likes and dislikes for the sake of more suitable planning.

This heart-to-heart communication lets messages be effectively exchanged, then each side is more able to understand the other's aims and means. Problems can be discussed and queries answered in time, as in a good partnership between people. The partners get to known each other superficially then gradually more deeply. Only if they are able to share their feelings openly and fully and to take each other properly into account can the relationship be harmonious and stable. If one of them lays the law down for the other, things are less likely to go smoothly.

Communication with animals in practice

As already mentioned, communication with animals is a kind of telepathy. Thoughts and feelings are effectively exchanged, though not through the medium of words. This is not an unusual experience between people who sympathize with each other and know each other well. The one partner may have a clear inkling of what is bothering the other without having to rely on interpreting words or deeds. Indeed, the expression *Great minds think alike!* is often used humorously to explain why the same odd suggestion is made by two friends at the same time. It is rather as if two series of waves move into phase and blend or as if two minds become one.

Brain activity can be measured and thoughts be observed in the form of waves, and some experts believe that even some animals are able to learn more about us in odd ways. Certainly dogs have been trained to scent and react to diabetes, once the concentration of sugar in the blood has risen above a certain limit. They are trained to recognize the limit, but the scenting is done naturally. As humans, we are often inclined to overlook ways of gathering information about the world if we ourselves rely on other ways. This also applies to telepathy, except that it seems to have no recourse to our five senses.

Telepathy is a different kind of communication altogether, and a person adept at communicating with animals has learned how to find the right plane of communication or how to resonate. He mainly ignores what he sees or hears, so as not to be misled. The right state is similar to a trance, and he has no need to face the animal or even to be in the same room or building, as the communication seems to be non-spatial and effective at any distance.

The communicator just has to feel as if he or she were together with the animal, which may explain to some extent why this kind of communication may even be used with animals now deceased but nonetheless clearly recalled by their former companions. The communication is not from body to body nor mainly an exchange of ideas but is rather a meeting of two spheres of awareness, each with its own nature.

One person who spread the notion of animal communication throughout the United States was Penelope Smith. She described this telepathic approach as like opening a channel directly between a person and an animal or like taking a portable phone out and phoning another person elsewhere for the sake of a chat. You send and receive messages as easily as if the other person were in front of you and nowadays you can do this even without a cable.

This is simply a handy illustration of how a message may be sent to an animal without any visible link. The message is sent specifically to one animal, then after a pleasant exchange, the call is ended, and the person and the animal go on separately with their lives.

The course of a communication

If you wish to put a call through to an animal, you need to have the right number, be it only metaphorically speaking. For communication at a distance, it is often useful to have a photo of the animal, ideally where the animal gazes into the camera, as this lets a communicator gaze into his eyes. As the saying goes, eyes are the windows of the soul, so these are an easy way in. Once the communicator feels in touch, he can ask specifically about the animal's age or past or whatever.

The preparation

If you wish to use the services of a professional communicator, you presumably want him to find out something specific about your animal by asking him relevant questions, so you have to tell him what you would like to know. Often, it is useful to ask for background information as well as specific details. After all, while someone is communicating with your animal, the communicator may be in no position to communicate with you.

Besides, animals may not reveal their secrets on demand or the secrets may not be the ones you are after. After all, the communication is more like a chat on the phone than like a police interrogation, and your priorities may not be the animal's, so what a communicator has in mind may not be in an animal's mind at the same time.

Suppose, for instance, that you would like to know more about an animal's state of health, it may be useful to let a communicator know what you have observed, be it only that an animal is behaving oddly. The communicator can then ask the animal why it has been doing so for no apparent reason, as if distressed. This may be more effective than just asking the animal whether or not he is feeling ill. After all, an animal may have no clear idea of illness in the medical sense, so the questions have to be limited to the range of the animal's notions and its replies be understood in the same terms.

In effect, it is quite a good idea to let a communicator with animals know something about your animal beforehand, but you may be loath to do so, as he may then rely on your input, not on messages from the animal.

Well, a communicator ought to ask an animal to 'say' more than *yes* or *no,* then any new information can be checked. Likewise, in chatting with other people, we expect them to do more than agree or disagree with what we are saying. An animal can offer unique information about himself, his relationship with you and his daily routine and even about your own habits and behavior. An animal may even offer details about his surroundings.

These may include details which you have not offered to the communicator and which he could hardly have guessed, unless they were offered by the animal, so if the communicator gives a faithful account of the communication, you then have reason to trust him. Of course, not all communicators are trustworthy, but the same is true of people in general.

If the problem is that an animal is missing, the communicator may initially gain information about the animals' feelings, such as anxiety, and also impressions of the animal's present surroundings. Not all impressions can be checked straightaway, so sometimes a communicator has to be trusted and a message believed for the time-being.

The communication as such

A photo is the usual link. A communicator can use it to identify the animal and to get in touch with it. To do so successfully, he has to calm himself down and to free his thoughts and feelings from the ballast of the day, which is rather like inducing a meditative or trance-like state. Shamans use the same procedure for invoking their power-animal on a spiritual plane.

In other words, the communicator prepares himself for getting in touch with the animal and for receiving messages and also tunes in to it sympathetically. This may be like opening the heart chakra, so the technique for opening the chakra may actually be used. There are no set rules or procedures. Some communicators use breathing techniques and others rely more on energy, as in focusing on a chakra. Some meditate, some fall into trances and some calm down in their own ways.

© depositphotos - michaeljung

Communicating with an animal, here with a horse for instance.

 83

A 'chat' with an animal can be thought of as being much like a chat with a human being. The communicator greets the animal, introduces himself and explains what he would like to learn. Every animal has its own personality and traits, so reactions vary from animal to animal. Like you, an animal may have its doubts about a communicator and be loath to cooperate, or the animal may welcome the opportunity and be open or even humorous. Its reaction may also depend on its present state. If in pain or anxious, desperate or frustrated, it is unlikely to react as if quite at ease.

All in all, the exchange is likely to vary from animal to animal, as it would from person to person, but finally a communicator has to come to the crunch and try to gain the relevant information. How questions are to be framed depends on the nature of the exchange and how it develops. In some cases, it is best for a communicator not to rush in and trample on sore toes, and in other cases, a communicator may be able to come straight to the point.

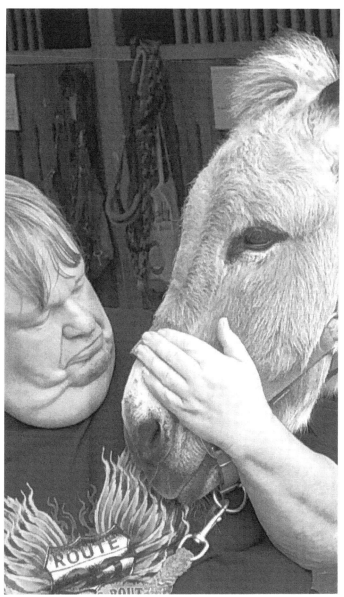

© Angela Fetzner

Here is my husband is interacting with our very ill and traumatized donkey Achiel, who requires a lot of patience.

 85

Among animals, as among humans, there are not only chatterboxes but also the tight-lipped, though the communication is not verbal. This too affects the course of communication. It an animal has a lot to make known and is keen to make it known, it may be hard for a communicator to keep its answers to the point, though of course, it is no easier with an animal loath to be candid. Between the extremes, there are many variants, so there are no set procedures.

This makes communication tricky but also more interesting, as it never becomes routine. A communicator with animals gets to know a whole range of other creatures, and however much experience he has had, there are always surprises in store.

The contents of communication

Since the communication is non-verbal and mind to mind, what are received are less often chains of ideas than single impressions. Just imagine that you have phoned a friend up and are chatting about the landscape in front of your window, though you are not gazing out at the time. You are less likely to list the plants or animals found in it than to recall and describe your visual impressions, the scents of the flowers and the songs of the birds. In general, most of the abstract notions in our minds are clad in sensual detail.

If you have twisted your ankle or hurt your leg, you may be less preoccupied with the medical name for your condition than with the difficulties you are having in walking up steps or in doing your daily chores. If you are chatting about a third person, she or he too is less likely in your imagination to be a name than a moving picture, which conjures up a whole range of feelings.

The same is true in communicating with an animal, except that the animal can communicate these images and feelings directly. The only things missing are the words, which we otherwise use to encode these images in messages.

Even in the case of small talk about the weather, we imagine the sun breaking through clouds, rain glittering on leaves, or wind blowing hats into the air. The words are often just labels attached to a whole range of personal images.

 87

There are not only images but also feelings, scents and other impressions, which a communicator may receive from an animal together with its thoughts. The impressions are conveyed from the depths of one mind to the depths of another then rise to the surface and may be experienced in much the same way as recalling a dream. The task is to put the images back together in such a way as to cast light on the matter at hand and to let the animal's owner benefit.

This does not imply that the impressions should be interpreted by the communicator. The latter should rather offer an owner a protocol or report, letting him know how well he was able to get through, how the animal reacted, what questions were posed, what impressions were conveyed, and how the communication fared as a whole.

If for instance a rather finicky cat is asked what kind of food it would prefer in future, the smell of fish might serve as an answer. A missing animal can often do little more than share impressions of its present surroundings or of what it has seen on the way, so the communication consists mainly of images.

If an animal is asked how it feels about its present surroundings or owner, the communication may rather consist of feelings.

Animals may not think as analytically as people, but a communicator may also receive answers in the form of words, just as his own thoughts often occur to him in this form. An animal's thoughts sometimes rise from the depths of his mind in the same way, and these are the kinds of impressions which are often the more surprising or humorous. This is due partly to the fact that some animals are able to think very clearly and to the point and to the fact impressions from the depths are often profound. If an animal is playful and tongue-in-cheek, its comments may be witty or ironic.

Misunderstandings are less likely to be due to fuzzy thought on the part of an animal than to human preconceptions in interpreting impressions. If a horse is asked if it is feeling fine, it may reply that it feels happy enough in a herd, or the question may conjure up in its mind happy memories of life in a herd. The communicator may then tell the owner that the horse is happy, when in fact it may be ill and lonely in its stall and be tired of being taken on walks alone.

Such misunderstandings are not reason enough to mistrust the communication as such.

The horse merely wished to 'say' that it would like to rejoin its herd, then the communicator took the wish to be present reality. The images were reliable but not the interpretation.

Hence, a communicator may have to be careful if offering the owner of an animal more than a series of impressions. In conveying the impressions, he may have to ask repeatedly whether or not they seem to make sense, and an owner may have to take into account the fact that not only a person but also an animal may express itself vaguely if unclear in its own mind.

A good communicator with animals may be aware of the pitfalls and try to make an owner aware of them too. By taking the nature and traits of an animal into account, the owner may more easily understand what it would like to convey, and this may pave the way to a better relationship.

Moreover, in knowing certain things about the animal already, he can pose tallying questions, to which he already knows the answers. This may help him to understand how the animal tries to express itself, then he can understand it better in future. In fact, mutual understanding may be easier than it sounds, and deep misunderstandings be uncommon. Humans and animals are able to share their thoughts and feelings, as they live in the same world in nearly the same way. The possibility of misunderstandings should merely be kept in mind.

© depositphotos - Istomin

Is the animal weary? Is the dog lonely? Might it be ill? It is not always easy to guess.

 91

Can we all communicate with animals?

All creatures have an inner life of some kind and they experience life in a similar way. The problem for a human being is to accept a shared level of communication and to be open to the experiences of a creature dissimilar in some respects, but this can be learned. Whatever helps you to relax and be open to new experiences is helpful in this respect, and whatever leads you to be critical or judgmental is a hindrance.

You may for instance find it helpful to go for a walk in the woods, to calm down and open your senses to new impressions or you may choose to meditate at home and learn how to focus on chakras. You may regain your inner balance by practicing yoga or by listening to restful music. Practice makes perfect, then you may be able to let the dust of activity settle, forget about the stress of daily life and become open to other impressions.

You may go to local lectures on communicating with animals or you may simply try it out for yourself by being open to an animal's thoughts and feelings. Any unusual impressions you then have may have come from the animal.

Sometimes we find it hard to communicate with even our own pets. If so, we may find it easier if we put aside our thoughts and feelings about them, but this is often more easily said than done, especially if a pet seems to be ill or has been at loggerheads with its owner for some time. But even in the face of such difficulties, communication may still be possible. Animals appreciate being addressed on a level they are able to respond on.

A person and an animal on the same wavelength

We sometimes say about ourselves and our friends that we are on the same wavelength or that our hearts beat as one. If you have ever tuned a violin or guitar, you know how it sounds and feels when a tuning fork and string are perfectly in tune. Not only every person but also every animal has its own energy and field of energy. The names for it differ from culture to culture but it is often called an aura. We all have auras, but not every aura has the same energy or frequency, intensity or hue.

If two creatures spend time together, they interact, have shared experiences of joy and sorrow and share and exchange energy. In the course of time, they may mingle more, revealing how well the partners know and accept each other and empathize with each other. They may then increasingly resonate with each other without losing their separate characteristics. On moving into phase, they become more harmonious.

Some of us are convinced that the animals entering our lives are those with whom we have a greater affinity. Some of us go even further in believing that animals come into our lives as mentors. This is the belief of shamans and similar people, who apply it to not only animals but also animal spirits, whom they treat as power animals. Some indigenous peoples revere a certain animal, whose energy and power they would like to share, and others have rituals to invoke it.

As regards power animals, each of us is thought to have a special affinity with a certain animal. This applies to not only an individual animal with its own particular temperament but also its group or species. The animal brings a certain vibration or frequency into a person's life and presents him with challenges or even riddles. Its particular energy revitalizes the person, if he is open to it and lets it enter him and cause him to resonate. It may help him to evolve further, gain new insights and become more fully a human being.

But a relationship with an animal is never one-sided, as an animal too may open itself up to a person and absorb his energy. As in the case of a conversation, both sides are affected by the exchange. The reciprocal nature of the relationship is what lets a person and an animal create a joint field of energy, as they adapt to each other, but this in itself is no guarantee of a harmonious relationship, as even if they are often at loggerheads, their energies continually interact. The aim of communication and understanding is not to make a person and an animal as alike as two peas in a pod, as each should remain true to its kind. It is rather that a deep, empathetic, trustful, affectionate and caring relationship lets their energies interact harmoniously and helps to resolve disagreements. Communication with an animal helps a person to understand any tension and to see the world through the animal's eyes. It lets the animal and its owner grow closer to each other and form a firm partnership. Even without words, this partnership may then survive through thick and thin.

© Michael Raab

Over more than two years I have developed a reliable feeling for my two donkeys. We understand one another.

 97

Epilogue

I began communicating with animals in the year 2018, on having saved two donkeys, Ahiel and Harrie, from slaughter in Belgium.

The two animals were severely traumatized from two years of suffering at a slaughterhouse. Animals are mostly passed on from one slaughterhouse to another for so long. Even in the period before this, their lives were certainly nothing to celebrate. One of the two donkeys, Achiel, was suffering from chronic obstructive bronchitis (COB), which has recently also been called equine asthma (EA).

I had already gone trekking with donkeys beforehand and had acquired a license to do so, but the two severely traumatized animals were still a great challenge for me and my husband.

By then, I was already very fond of donkeys, being impressed by their strength of will, their even tempers, their intelligence, their intuition and their attentiveness. If ever I had a chance, I visited donkey retreats and sanctuaries at home and abroad.

Hence, on coming face to face with the two donkeys about to be slaughtered through ingratitude, I felt an urgent need for action.

If you think that it must be easy to take a horse or donkey across a border in the European Union, you had better think again. The rules and regulations are very strict. The animals have to be officially examined and transported in a certified vehicle. The costs involved are much more than the costs of buying the animals.

At first, it was hard for us to persuade the donkeys to accept us. Both of them had learned that they could rely only on each other and ought not to trust anyone else. Above all, they had learned never to trust people, as life with them had never been pleasant.

They would snap at and bite us at the least provocation and give anyone else a wide berth or kick out at them. They were not even soothed by being stroked or brushed, and putting a halter or blanket on either of them was enough to fray anyone's nerves.

Certainly, they appreciated being taken for walks, but on meeting any other people, they would often panic, back away and try to stay at a distance.

We soon realized that trying to get along with big animals can be a considerable and risky challenge.

Moreover, Achiel's health continually worsened, though we left no stone unturned in trying to help him. The veterinary surgeon examined him nearly every day and he had to be taken to hospital. We rented a brine car and made life for the donkey less arduous with the help of cortisone inhalation and occasionally cortisone injections. We also tried various herbs for the bronchi and carried out tests for allergies. Nothing produced a lasting cure. Achiel became weaker and gaunter from day to day.

My husband and I finally took courses in communicating with animals. Achiel let my husband know that he was not yet ready to pass on and would like to spend a few happy years with us and Harrie.

One day, Achiel ate nothing, and the veterinary surgeon said that she would have to put him to sleep at once or the following week. It would make little difference, but Achiel let my husband know that he was keen to hold on. We then took him without hesitation to the University Clinic in Gießen, where he was found to have an oxygen saturation of only 42%, not the normal saturation of 98%. the veterinary surgeon in the clinic said that a donkey in such a state should hardly be allowed to stand and had little chance of recovery.

The next day another veterinary surgeon looked after him and promised not to give up on him. In a remarkably short time, Achiel got better and is now a merry and happy donkey, full of energy and zest.

His recovery shows that there are some things between heaven and earth which cannot be explained rationally and that sometimes experimental measurements such as the percentage of oxygen do not fully reflect an animal's condition.

Achiel's unconquerable will to live proved all the medics and skeptics to be wrong. He had let us know clearly enough that he was not going to waste his opportunity.

By now, the donkeys let themselves be stroked and brushed, are mostly even willing to be cuddled and are satisfied and well balanced donkeys.

Nevertheless, their past sometimes catches up with them again and they fall victim to their anxieties, but we are now confident that we shall be able to develop an even deeper relationship with our donkeys by communicating with them suitably.

I hope that you, my readers, will likewise be able to develop deep and trusting relationships with your animals and in the course of time will be able to overcome any difficulties.

About the author

Dr. Angela Fetzner was born and grew up in Bad Kissingen in Germany. Since 1996 she has been working as a pharmacist in public and hospital pharmacies, mainly in Germany and Switzerland, and has also held seminars throughout Europe.

She qualified as a pharmacist at the Julius Maximilian University in Würzburg, went on to work for two years in a public pharmacy in the north of Germany and finally undertook postgraduate studies in the history of pharmacy at Philipps University in Marburg, gaining a doctorate (Dr. rer. Nat.).

As a trained pharmacist with useful specialized knowledge, she delights in making complex medical issues widely intelligible and since 2012 has published more than 50 guidebooks and textbooks, many of which are about healthcare and have inspired hundreds of thousands of readers.

In her spare time, she loves to withdraw into nature and to go for long walks with her donkeys, Achiel and Harrie, whom she saved from the slaughterhouse.

Von 2012-2020 Veröffentlichung von mehr als 50 Ratgebern und Fachbüchern v. a. zu verschiedenen Gesundheitsthemen, die Hunderttausende von Lesern begeistern.

© Michael Raab

Dr. Angela Fetzner with her donkey „Harrie"

A heartfelt thank you

is due at this point to all my esteemed readers. If my guide has been satisfying and useful to you, I would appreciate a short review. Praise, blame or suggestions can be left on my Facebook page:

https://www.facebook.com/AngelaFetzner

or on my homepage as an author:
https://www.angela-fetzner.de

Books from Dr. Angela Fetzner
are likewise all to be found on my homepage as an author:
https://www.angela-fetzner.de
I would also like to offer my readers a special service. My online readings are regularly announced on my homepage, where book reviews and blog articles appear too. On it, you may sign up for my newsletter for regular information about new books, promotions and raffles as well as health tips.
My e-books are in all the leading online stores, and my printed books are in the mail order and standard book trade. I myself am on the social networks: Facebook, Twitter, Instagram and

Youtube: https://angela-fetzner.de//

More books from Dr. Angela Fetzner

Dr. Angela Fetzner

The Lymph

The Body's Purification Plant

Lymphatic cleansing

This has become the stepchild of all detoxification therapy. Cleansing of the liver or colon is high on the agenda, but detoxification of the lymphatic system is often neglected. Regular detoxification of the lymphatic system is nonetheless crucial for physical and mental health.

The lymphatic system

This is the body's purification plant, ridding it of whatever is harmful or useless like pathogens, metabolic waste, toxins and cell debris. It is crucial for immunity and the body's detoxification.

Sustaining the flow

The lymphatic system must be regularly cleansed and detoxified to keep on flowing naturally. If continually overloaded with waste, it stagnates. The system can no longer get rid of all problematic materials, so these gradually poison the whole body and often cause chronic ailments.

Lymphatic cleansing

This book outlines all natural therapies and treatments which have proven to be effective in basic lymphatic detoxification and cleansing. These everyday ways to look after yourself are motivating and efficient. They include approaches like medicinal plant therapy, homeopathy, Schuessler salts, specific cleansing of the lymph, water applications, stress reduction, changes of diet, moderate exercise and so on. With the help of these choice means of detoxification, you will soon feel livelier, stronger and merrier.

As a doctor of pharmacology, the author has been advising and informing clients for more than two decades, being committed to their health and well being.

Your pharmacist, Angela Fetzner

Dr. Angela Fetzner

Power Animals & Shamanism

Finding the Lost Soul

Regaining a lost soul

In this book, the millennia-old healing techniques of shamanism are presented clearly and appealingly. The book is meant to give readers an overview of the complex and manifold facets of shamanism and to encourage them to reach out to their respective power animal.

Power animals – spiritual companions and leaders

Power animals are spiritual companions and soulmates, and each has a personal relationship with its human counterpart, who is thereby empowered, energized, deepened and motivated. The person is enabled to find his or her true purpose, to develop more fully and to avoid pitfalls, is protected, kept healthy and even healed, and can turn to the animal for help at any time. The more he or she does so, the more intense their partnership becomes. Some partnerships last a lifetime.

How do you find your power animal?

This book explains how to find, honor and bond with your power animal and thereby be strengthened and healed. It explains how the animal may be lost and how the loss may be averted.

The main power animals

The most important power animals and their meaning and message for humans are discussed in detail, revealing what positive qualities may be transferred from one to you.

The worldview of shamanism

This book offers all key information about shamanism and how to use it. The division of the shamanic cosmos into the upper, middle and lower worlds is explained, as are details of shamanic journeys. The role of the master of animals in particular is examined, as is the difference between spirit helpers and totem animals. The basic features of neo-shamanism are shown too.

Dr. Angela Fetzner

Detoxification
Heal, Strengthen, Let Go

Detoxification – the removal of pollutants from the body – can look back on a long tradition.

Since time immemorial, people have felt a wish to cleanse their bodies and souls at regular intervals and to rid them of needless and harmful ballast. This may be due to the instinctive feeling that purification is a great relief for body and soul and is also needed to maintain or regain health. At the same time, a thorough detoxification and cleansing of the body is a prerequisite for all deeper processes of healing.

Among other things, detoxification measures are used to activate the body's powers of self-healing. Only by thoroughly removing pollutants can we remove the precondition for many ailments, letting body and soul recover.

This book describes all natural therapies which have proven to be effective in basic detoxification. These measures are down to earth, motivating and efficient and include medicinal plant therapy, homeopathy, Schuessler salts, specific cleansing of the organs of detoxification, water applications, wraps, reduction of stress, changes of diet and so on.

With the help of the detoxification cures here chosen and presented, you will soon regain your vitality, strength and zeal.

With kind regards from your pharmacist, Dr. Angela Fetzner

Dr. Angela Fetzner

The wonders of woodland

Woodland – a contemplative site

Exposed to a flood of sensory impressions and an ever faster pace, more and more of us are finding it hard to switch off and relax, but at the same time, there is an ever growing need to slow down and recover.

The more we yield to the burden of multitasking and succumb to the stress of hobbies and rushing around, the more we need an alternative and counterweight to the challenge of modern times.

As life becomes more hectic and demanding, we often long only to let go, empty our minds and let ourselves drift.

Too many appointments, rivalry at work and strife in the family – far too often we are caught in the treadmill of must and should.

In woodland, we are free to roam and dream without any obligations and to observe without interfering. We can impartially let it affect us and note the effects.

There is no competition or pressure to stand out in woodland; there is no agitation or deadline to be met.

We leave the vicious circle of doubt and reflection, and instead we feel and live in the present, in the here and now.

We escape the vortex of negative thoughts and worries, and the primal force of woodland takes over, offering us sustenance, strength and consolation.

Our hearts dilate, our minds become free, and we change from thinking to feeling. We breathe the power of the woodland in without impairing the woodland in any way.

Nature draws us away from our worries, vexations and problems, and our minds focus on nature and trees, becoming more attentive and meditative.

The book contains numerous colored photos and illustrations

Printed in Great Britain
by Amazon